Following Jesus

Helping you and your family discover more about Jesus

30 Devotions

70 Activities

4 Pathways

Sarah
GRACE
PUBLISHING
Dyslexic Friendly

First published 2022 by Sarah Grace Publishing, an imprint of
Malcolm Down Publishing Ltd.
www.malcolmdown.co.uk

25 24 23 22   7 6 5 4 3 2 1

British Library Cataloguing-in-Publication Data
A catalogue record for this book is available from the British Library.

ISBN 978-1-912863-94-5

Cover design by Gail Hanks at Duckhouse Design

Printed in the UK

Contents

Introduction

Bible verse: Matthew 4:19

Jesus said, 'Come follow me.'

The Bible is a *big* book and it can be difficult to know where to begin. Discovering more about Jesus is a great place to start! From the creation of the universe to the present day and beyond, Jesus is at the centre of it all.

Whether you have been following Jesus for years or you are wondering who Jesus is, *Next Steps to Following Jesus* is a flexible and engaging resource that helps children and families at all stages of faith to walk through the Bible and explore the life of Jesus together. Here, you'll find out more about Jesus, what he did during his time on earth and why he is at the heart of the Bible.

As well as reading about the extraordinary life of Jesus, you can enjoy adventures along four different pathways that bring the life of Jesus into the life of your family. You can choose one pathway or try them all.

We hope that you enjoy *Next Steps to Following Jesus* and discover new and exciting things about him that encourage you and your family to love and live for God.

With love from
Joanne and Shell

Four Pathways

Jesus said that the greatest commandment is to love the Lord your God with all your mind, heart, **strength** and **soul** (see Mark 12:30 and Luke 10:27). *Next Steps to Following Jesus* includes activities to involve your family in applying all four.

The **THINK** pathway helps you to engage your brain to work things out. Connect with God by fact-finding and using your mind.

The **FEEL** pathway aids in building connections between the head and heart. Be with God in the silence and enjoy the wonders of creation.

The **GET ACTIVE** pathway encourages you to do something practical and to put words into action. See God at work as you get stuck in.

The **CREATE** pathway inspires you to make, bake and express your creativity. Experience God in the here and now.

Jesus in Creation

Bible verses: John 1:1-4

Before the world began, there was the Word. The Word was with God, and the Word was God. He was with God in the beginning. All things were made through him. Nothing was made without him. In him there was life.

Jesus came to earth as a human being when he was born in Bethlehem, but he existed long before that. In fact, there is no moment in history when Jesus did not exist.

In John 1:1, Jesus is called the Word. Jesus was with God when all things were made. When God created the world, Jesus was with him. When God created man and woman, Jesus was there. Why? Because Jesus is God. He will always be and has always been, even before the beginning began. How awesome is that?

If you're finding all of this a bit too much to take in, don't worry. We're not meant to understand God completely. If we could fully understand the mystery of God, he wouldn't be God! The most important thing to know is that true life is found in Jesus.

When we make the choice to follow Jesus, we become friends with the one and only all-powerful, all-knowing, forever-faithful God, who loves us more than we could ever imagine.

Read More About It

in **Genesis 1.** Imagine Jesus being there as the world was made.

THINK: Read 2 Timothy 1:9 and Titus 1:2. Which phrase is repeated? What does this tell you about Jesus?

FEEL: Take off your shoes and walk barefoot on the grass or the sand, in the ocean or even on some soil or mud. Get close to the things God has created.

GET ACTIVE: Go stargazing. Wrap up warmly, grab some blankets and look up at the stars. See the wonder that God has made. You could even make a camp fire and toast marshmallows.

The Trinity:
Three in One

Bible verse: 2 Corinthians 13:14

*The grace of the Lord Jesus Christ, the love
of God, and the fellowship of the Holy Spirit
be with you all.*

Did you know that God the Father, God the Son and God the
Holy Spirit make up the one, true God? They are three, equal
persons and none could exist without the others. This one
God of three persons is known as the Trinity.

God the Father is the Creator of all things and the Father of
all people. He is the First Person of the Trinity. God the Father
cares for his creation and wants to protect and provide for it.
He has a deep love for everything he has made.

God the Son is Jesus, the Second Person of the Trinity. Jesus
lived on earth for a while as God in the form of a human. He
helps us to understand God's amazing love for us. He gives life
in all its fullness to those who choose to follow him.

Then last, but not least, is **God the Holy Spirit**, the Third
Person of the Trinity. Through his power everything was made
in Jesus, *by* God. The Holy Spirit is God in us, helping us to
know God's presence every day.

Together, the Father, Jesus and the Holy Spirit make up the
one, true God.

Read More About It

in **Matthew 3:13-17**. Notice how God the Father, God the Son and God the Holy Spirit are all present in some way.

THINK: Try this science experiment. Get three cups. Fill one cup with ice, one cup with water and one cup with steam. (Try putting a glass in the fridge to make it cold, then breathe into it, filling it with condensation to make it look like it's full of steam. Make sure you ask a grown-up to help you if you use real steam. It's very hot!) All are H_2O (water) in different forms. How does this help you to understand the Trinity?

FEEL: A long time ago, St Patrick used a clover to explain the Trinity to the Irish people. Spend a few moments looking at this image. How does it help you to understand the concept of the Trinity?

CREATE: Collect three pieces of ribbon, wool or string in three different colours. Plait them together so that the three become one. Tie a knot at each end and use the plait as a bookmark, a bracelet or a bag tie to remind you that God is three persons in one.

God's Rescue Plan

Bible verse: Genesis 3:15

*I will make you and the woman
enemies to each other.
Your descendants and her descendants
will be enemies.
Her child will crush your head.
And you will bite his heel.*

The Bible teaches that, in the beginning, God made the world to be *very good*. But human beings messed it up. We forgot who we were made to be.

All humans are made in God's image, but we are not God. We can make good and bad choices, but only God is truly good all the time.

Whenever people decide to ignore God, it leads to things that are *not* good. Things such as selfishness, greed, pride, vanity and laziness are what the Bible calls 'sin'. Sin is what happens when we make something else more important to us than God.

Ignoring God ▸ Making bad choices ▸ Sin ▸ Hurt and suffering ▸ Needing a Saviour

Even though humans had made a mess of things, God immediately made a plan to save us. He said a child would crush the head of God's enemy – but the act of crushing would also hurt. Which child grew up to save all humans in a way that was painful but ultimately defeated sin and all the enemies of God? Jesus!

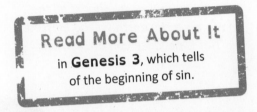

Read More About It
in **Genesis 3**, which tells of the beginning of sin.

FEEL: Collect some beautiful and some broken things from nature (feathers, leaves, bark and so on) to remind you of the goodness of God's creation and the effect of sin on the natural world.

GET ACTIVE: Sometimes sin is described as falling short or missing the target of God's best for us. Create a game in which you have to throw or kick balls across a line and into a bucket or basket. Assign someone to be 'Jesus', who picks up all the balls that have fallen short or missed the basket and puts them in for you. How many did you get into the basket? How many did 'Jesus' have to put in for you? (If you're short of space, you could play this game with jelly beans and a cup.)

The Family History of Jesus

You may already know that Jesus had a mother called Mary who married Joseph. Together, they raised Jesus from a baby to a grown man. But did you know that Jesus' family was much bigger and more intriguing than just Mary and Joseph?

For centuries, God chose certain men and women to be part of Jesus' family tree. If you dare, you can read the whole list of his family members in two gospels: Matthew 1:1-16 and Luke 3:23-38.

Matthew traces Jesus' family tree from Joseph's father all the way back to Abraham, who may have lived at some time between 2100 and 1900 BC. Luke, it seems, traces Jesus' ancestors from Joseph's father-in-law all the way back to the first human who ever lived – Adam.

God made a special promise to Abraham. He said he would bless every nation on earth through his descendants (that means his family born after him). Those descendants became known as the Israelites (later called Jews) and Jesus was one of them.

So two thousand years *before* Jesus was born, God was already preparing the way for him.

Read More About It

in **Acts 3:11-26**, which explains how Jesus is the fulfilment of God's promise to Abraham.

FEEL: Think about all the people who have ever stood on, sat in or walked through the spot where you are right now – ten years ago, a hundred years ago or a thousand years ago. Jesus walked in the same places as Abraham. What must that have felt like?

CREATE: Here are the most famous people from Jesus' family tree. Circle all the names you recognise and choose one to draw a picture of – what might that person have looked like?

Mary, Joseph, Jesus
King Hezekiah, King Josiah
King Solomon and his mother Bathsheba
King David, the son of Jesse
Boaz, his mother Rahab and his wife Ruth
Judah, the father of Perez, whose mother was Tamar
Abraham, Isaac, Jacob
Shem, the son of Noah
Lamech, Methuselah, Enoch
Seth, the son of Adam, the first man

The Prophecies:
Jesus' Birth

Bible verse: Isaiah 9:6

A child will be born to us.
God will give a son to us.
He will be responsible for leading the people.
His name will be Wonderful Counselor, Powerful God,
Father Who Lives Forever, Prince of Peace.

God had many things to say to his people, the Israelites, so he gave messages, called prophecies, to certain people known as 'prophets'. A prophet would deliver these messages publicly and, sometimes, in very embarrassing ways to get people's attention (such as walking around naked for three years*).

A prophecy is like a signpost. When Jesus grew up, people were not sure who he was. The prophecies about his birth helped them to believe that he was the Christ, the chosen one, the Son of God – a gift from God to us.

The detail within these 'signposts' is amazing. For example, Jesus was born in Bethlehem (known as the town of David) and lived for a while in Egypt but grew up in Nazareth, which fulfilled three of the prophecies about him. Isn't that remarkable?

Read More About It

in **Luke 1:30-33**; **Isaiah 11:1**; **Isaiah 20***; **Hosea 11:1**; and **Micah 5:2**.

THINK: There are lots of little signposts on the previous page. Use a ruler to draw a line from each signpost in the direction it is pointing. Where do the lines meet? This tells you what they are pointing to.

GET ACTIVE: Use natural objects in your garden or a park (twigs, leaves and so on) to make a path of arrows leading to a hiding place. Ask someone to follow them to find you or some hidden treasure.

15

The Prophecies:
Jesus' Purpose

Bible verse: Isaiah 61:1

The Lord God has put his Spirit in me.
This is because he has appointed me to tell the good
news to the poor.
He has sent me to comfort those whose hearts are broken.
He has sent me to tell the captives they are free.
He has sent me to tell the prisoners that they are released.

During his time on the earth, Jesus had a clear purpose that was planned long before he arrived. Hundreds of years before Jesus was born, a prophet named Isaiah spoke and wrote about the Messiah (a title given to Jesus) who would be sent by God. The Messiah would carry God's Spirit within him and do incredible things, including preaching the message of God (the good news) to those who needed to hear it (which is pretty much everyone). He would help hurting and sad people, and offer freedom to anyone who felt trapped.

Isaiah was God's mouthpiece and he told the Israelites about what was to come. It all sounded very exciting.

Here's something else that's exciting: the Bible tells us about the time when Jesus was invited to read part of Isaiah's message from some scrolls. Guess which bit Jesus read? His own job description – the same words that Isaiah had written hundreds of years before, which we can read in Isaiah 61. Wow!

16

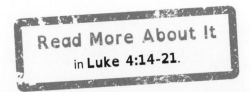

Read More About It
in **Luke 4:14-21**.

FEEL: Your purpose is often linked to the things you are good at or enjoy doing. What could your purpose be? Spend some time thinking about the things you love to do and ask God to show you, in his own time, how these things might be a part of your future. Stay alert for God's response.

CREATE: Find a piece of plain, white paper and some tea bags. Soak the tea bags in water and then rub them on the paper. Once the paper is dry, write the words from Isaiah 61:1 on it and roll it up to create your own scroll.

The lord has put His Spirit in me

The Prophecies:
Jesus' Death

Bible verse: Isaiah 53:6

We all have wandered away like sheep.
Each of us has gone his own way.
But the Lord has put on him the punishment
for all the evil we have done.

The Bible verse likens evil or sin to going our own way, instead of God's way. God described his way in laws given to the Israelites through a man called Moses. You might have heard of the first ten laws – they are known as the Ten Commandments. However, God knew that it was impossible for everyone to follow all the laws all the time. He knew that everyone sometimes 'goes astray' and follows their own way instead of his way. So, at the same time, God gave people a way to deal with the problem of sin.

At first, that way was to sacrifice animals at the Temple in Jerusalem. The animal would be an offering to God that was a way of saying sorry to him. But animal sacrifices had to be made every single year because they were only a temporary solution to the problem of sin.

Isaiah prophesied that, one day, someone would come to deal with the problem of sin forever. That person would never do anything wrong. Rather, he would willingly sacrifice himself so that the rest of the world might be forgiven once and for all.

That person is Jesus. He took the punishment for all the wrong things we have done (and all the wrongs things we will do in the future) when he died on the cross. Even though each one of us has wandered away from God, Jesus himself became 'The Way' back to God. He solved the problem of sin forever and put us on the right path.

> **Read More About It**
> in all of **Isaiah 53** and
> **Hebrews 7:18-27** and **10:9-10**.

THINK: Look up the Ten Commandments in Exodus 20 (in the International Children's Bible if you have it) and fill in the blanks:

1. You must not have any other _____ except me.
2. You must not make any _____.
3. You must not use the _____ of God _____.
4. Keep the _____ as a holy day.
5. Honour your _____ and your _____.
6. You must not _____ anyone.
7. You must not be _____ of adultery.
8. You must not _____ .
9. You must not tell _____ about your neighbour.
10. You must not want to take anything that belongs to your _____.

Turn the page – there's more!

CREATE: Using playdough, make a cross like the one Jesus died on. You could also have a go at making the sheep referred to in the Bible verse and Jesus too. To make your own playdough, follow this simple recipe:

2 mugs of plain flour
2 mugs of water
1 mug of salt
4 tsp cream of tartar
2 tbsp oil
Your favourite food colouring

Stir the ingredients together in a saucepan on a low-to-medium heat until they are well mixed. Once the mixture has cooled, it's ready to use.

Jesus Is Born

Bible verses: Luke 2:11-12

Today your Saviour was born in David's town. He is Christ, the Lord. This is how you will know him: You will find a baby wrapped in cloths and lying in a feeding box.

You would expect the birth of Jesus to take place in a royal palace. After all, he was the greatest king ever to have been born on Planet Earth. But not this king. In fact, Jesus' birth was unique.

God chose Mary, an unmarried teenager, to be Jesus' mother. Jesus was born where the smelly animals lived, in the backstreets of Bethlehem. There weren't the usual celebrations. Instead, to announce the arrival of Jesus, the newborn King, God sent an angel to some poor, lowly shepherds. He also sent a star for a group of stargazers (wise men) to follow. Jesus' cot was a feeding box full of hay, his first blanket was strips of cloth and he was visited by strangers.

But . . . Jesus' birth was a very *big* deal, and it was part of a really *big* plan.

He had come to save the world and bring people back to God. All the events surrounding Jesus' birth happened because God wanted them to happen that way. Yes, Jesus was the Son of God, the Saviour, the Light of the World, but he didn't need a royal welcome. He was going to change people's lives through showing God's love in a way that had not been seen before.

Jesus was born more than two thousand years ago but, all over the world, people still celebrate his birth each year at Christmas time. That's why it's called '*Christ*-mas'. God's rescue plan for mankind had begun.

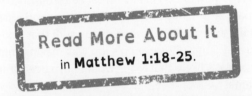

Read More About It
in **Matthew 1:18-25**.

FEEL: Find an old piece of cloth, some straw and a wooden or metal box. Feel their textures. What would it be like for a baby to have those materials around them? Next, find a soft blanket, a cushion and a basket. What would it be like for a baby to have those materials around them?

CREATE: Make your own nativity scene. You could paint stones, use playdough, draw a picture, raid the recycling bin, or use leaves and twigs or building blocks. Think about where Jesus was born and who was there.

Jesus as a Child

Bible verse: Luke 2:52

Jesus continued to learn more and more and to grow physically. People liked him, and he pleased God.

We hear lots about Jesus as a baby and as a fully grown man, but it can be easy to forget that Jesus was a child too. While he was growing up, he would have felt many of the things that you feel.

Jesus spent his childhood in a town called Nazareth in Galilee. He was part of a family and he had brothers and sisters. His mum, Mary, and stepdad, Joseph, made sure that God was at the centre of family life. Joseph's job was making things out of wood and it's likely that Jesus would have been trained to do the same.

Jesus would have learned how to walk, talk and use the toilet. He would have fallen over and grazed his knee. He would have learned how to read and write. He would have laughed and cried, felt sad and happy, and loved and lost. He was fully God and fully human at the same time, making him an ordinary human being with extraordinary wisdom, understanding and knowledge of God. Jesus knew why he was here on the earth, and he was determined to do everything that God had sent him to do.

Jesus didn't start teaching and healing in public until he was thirty years old. Everything that happened in his childhood taught him life lessons, preparing him for his future and all that was yet to come.

Read More About It

in **Luke 2:41-52**, which tells us about Jesus when he was twelve years old.

FEEL: Make a list of things that babies, toddlers and children can experience as they grow up. Think about some of the emotions they might have. You could use your own experiences to help you. What's it like knowing that Jesus had similar feelings and experienced similar things when he was a child?

GET ACTIVE: When Jesus was a child, it's very likely that he played games such as draughts and chess. He might have also played ball games with a leather or string ball. He may have played 'mums and dads' or 'swords and slings', or with spinning tops and other wooden toys. As a family, play a game similar to one Jesus might have played. Which game did you choose?

CREATE: Print off some photos taken of you while you were growing up. Include treasured memories and milestones. Make a collage with your photos and frame it or stick it on your bedroom wall. Do this as a way of remembering special moments in your childhood, just as the Bible records special moments in Jesus' life.

Jesus Is Baptised

Bible verses: Luke 3:21-22

When all the people were being baptised by John, Jesus also was baptised. While Jesus was praying, heaven opened and the Holy Spirit came down on him. The Spirit was in the form of a dove. Then a voice came from heaven and said, 'You are my Son and I love you. I am very pleased with you.'

The first public act Jesus ever did was not to heal someone or teach a parable. The first thing he did was to be baptised by his cousin, John the Baptist, in the River Jordan. As soon as that happened, the Holy Spirit came down onto Jesus and the voice of his Father, God, was heard speaking over him.

Baptism is something Christians do to show the world that they want to follow Jesus. For a Christian, it *means* something important. It means that you are washing away your old life and the wrong choices you have made. It also means saying yes to following Jesus and starting a fresh, new life with him.

Baptism often happens after someone becomes a Christian for the first time or becomes old enough to choose to follow Jesus for themselves. Additionally, parents might baptise or dedicate their babies in church, wanting their child to be blessed by God, just as Jesus was.

Read More About It
in **Matthew 3** and
Acts 2:38-47 and **19:1-4**.

THINK: Have you been baptised? If not, do you think you might want to be baptised? As a family, share any stories of baptism that you may have.

CREATE: Find a square piece of paper and create your own origami dove using the instructions below.

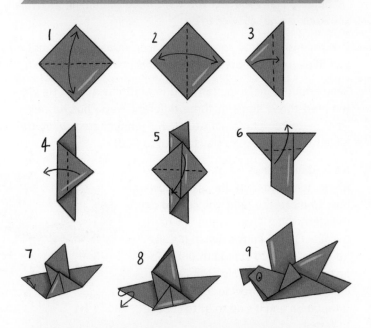

GET ACTIVE: Have a race with your paper doves.

Jesus Is Tempted

Bible verse: Matthew 4:1

*Then the Spirit led Jesus into the desert
to be tempted by the devil.*

'Tempted' means you feel you want to do something that you know you are not allowed to do.

Everyone is tempted sometimes – even Jesus was. It is not a bad thing to be tempted. What matters is what you do next.

Read about Jesus being tempted in Matthew 4:1-11. He was tempted three times in three different ways, but he never gave in to temptation. Instead, he remembered what the Bible said and chose to stay faithful to God.

Jesus understands what it feels like to be tempted, but he also knows how to make the right choice and do the right thing, even when it's hard. Because Jesus knows what it's like, he can help us to stay faithful to God just as *he* did. The Bible promises that God will always provide a way out of temptation and it's up to us to choose to take it.

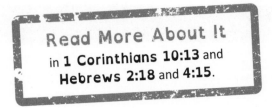

Read More About It
in **1 Corinthians 10:13** and
Hebrews 2:18 and **4:15**.

Jesus Is Tempted

THINK: Here is a scale from 1 to 10. Write or draw things on the scale that you find tempting (you can be silly or serious). It might be stealing biscuits from the biscuit tin or being mean to someone who annoys you. What does it feel like to be tempted? How does it change as you move along the scale?

1   5   10

(Not very tempting)   (Extremely tempting)

GET ACTIVE: Choose your favourite sweets or biscuits. Put them on a plate in an area of your house where everyone in your family will see them. Place a sign in front of them saying 'Do Not Eat'. How long will the treats stay on the plate before someone gives in to temptation and eats them? How long can you hold out for?

Do Not Eat!

29

Jesus Says, 'Follow Me'

Bible verses: Mark 1:17-18

Jesus said to them, 'Come and follow me. I will make you fishermen for men.' So Simon and Andrew immediately left their nets and followed him.

Jesus' first job, as he stepped into his God-given purpose, was to choose some people who would follow him and become his friends. He knew how important it is to have good friends.

Jesus invited Simon and Andrew to follow him. Straight away, without question, they stopped what they were doing and followed him. They weren't going to miss out on being friends with Jesus.

Simon and Andrew spent most of their time with Jesus. They were part of a group of twelve people known as Jesus' disciples. As well as being their friend, Jesus taught the disciples about God and how to live in the way God wanted them to live. He also taught them how to tell others about God so that many more people would believe and be saved.

When you choose to follow Jesus, you become one of his disciples too. You learn to live how Jesus lived, putting God first in everything you do. Following Jesus isn't always easy. There will be times when it is the hardest thing to do but don't be afraid. God promises always to be with you and to help you along the way.

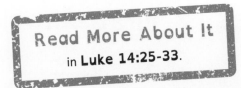

Read More About It
in **Luke 14:25-33**.

FEEL: Jesus' followers eventually became his closest friends. Who are your friends and how do they make you feel? Do they build you up or bring you down? What makes a good friend? Jesus is the best kind of friend you could ever have.

GET ACTIVE: Use some household objects to set up an indoor or outdoor assault course. You can make it as easy or as difficult as you like. Next, put a blindfold on a member of your family and guide them from one end of the assault course to the other, using only words.

CREATE: Choose a piece of orchestral music and sit down with a large, blank piece of paper and a pencil. As the music is playing, close your eyes, hold the pencil in your hand and make marks on the paper that follow the music. For example, if the music is flowing you might draw smooth, curvy marks on your paper. If the music is loud, you might draw bold, heavy marks. When you have finished, you could colour in parts of your picture and turn it into a piece of art – or even a masterpiece.

Jesus' First Miracle

Bible verse: John 2:11

*So in Cana of Galilee, Jesus did his first miracle.
There he showed his glory, and his followers
believed in him.*

Jesus, his mother, Mary, and his friends had been invited to a wedding in a town called Cana in Galilee. There, the wine had run out. So Jesus asked for six huge, stone jars to be filled with ordinary water. When the guests came to drink the water, it had turned into wine, and not just any old wine – it was the finest wine. Jesus was the one who turned the water into wine and his friends and followers were amazed.

This was Jesus' first miracle. He was thirty years old when it happened. Jesus didn't perform miracles to show off. He did it to illustrate how powerful and glorious God is. He did it to help people and reveal the love of God to those who were in need. Everything Jesus did was about showing others how good God is.

The miracles of Jesus give us a small glimpse of what is to come in heaven. They also remind us of God's original plan for our world. It was supposed to be a place where there was no pain, no sickness, no hunger and no disease.

The greatest miracle *ever* took place when Jesus' died on the cross, was buried in a tomb and then came back to life! That miracle still has the power to change people's lives forever because it makes it possible for us to be friends with God.

Read More About It

in the **Bible**, where there are lots of stories of Jesus' performing miracles. Read about two more miracles in **John 6:1-21**.

THINK: Read the full story of Jesus' turning water into wine (John 2:1-11). Make a list of all the people who are mentioned. Which of these people knew Jesus had performed the miracle? Which of them didn't? What does this tell you about Jesus?

GET ACTIVE: Ask one member of your family to pour out different types of drink (juice, water, milk, pop and so on) into cups. The other members of your family can take it in turns to wear a blindfold and guess which drink is in each cup. You could make it harder by using different brands or versions of the same juice or different types of milk to see who can tell the difference.

Jesus Heals

Bible verses: John 9:1-3

As Jesus was walking along, he saw a man who had been born blind. His followers asked him, 'Teacher, whose sin caused this man to be born blind – his own sin or his parents' sin?'

Jesus answered . . . 'This man was born blind so that God's power could be shown in him.'

There are lots of stories in the Bible that prove God can heal people. Jesus healed a blind man, he brought people back to life and he made it possible for people to walk again.

God's healing comes in all different shapes and sizes. It can happen straight away, over time or it can seem as if it will never happen at all. One thing we can be sure of – God can heal. There are many people all over the world who have experienced or seen God's healing power in action. When God does heal, it's a glimpse of what is to come in heaven.

Some things seem impossible, but God makes all things possible. That doesn't mean we always understand how or why God heals people in the way he does. It means that we can have faith and believe in God's healing power for our family and friends.

Jesus healed people because he believed in the power of God that lived within him. That same power is in us. When we pray in the name of Jesus for people to be healed, amazing things can happen. When people are healed, God's power is on display for all to see.

Read More About It

in **Luke 8:40-55**, which tells how Jesus healed a woman and a twelve-year-old girl.

THINK: Try this memory game. Fill a tray with medical or first-aid items, such as plasters, bandages, antiseptic cream, a medicine spoon and a thermometer. Look at the items on the tray for sixty seconds, try to memorise them and then cover them up. Who can remember the most items on the tray? These things help us to heal and get better, but Jesus is the ultimate healer.

FEEL: Jesus often healed people by laying his hands on them. On a piece of blank paper, draw around your hand(s) and write the names of people you know who need God to heal them. Each day, pray for God to heal those people.

Jesus Forgives

Bible verse: Matthew 9:2

*Jesus saw that these people had great faith,
so he said to the paralysed man, 'Be happy,
young man. Your sins are forgiven.'*

In Jesus' day, the Jewish leaders knew that only God had the power to forgive sins. When we sin, we are doing something wrong against God. That's why it's God who must forgive us. When Jesus forgave the sins of the paralysed man, Jesus was saying that he was equal with God.

Forgiveness is wonderful. It's like taking a warm bath after you've fallen in the mud or like walking again when you've been paralysed. It's new hope, new life and a fresh start.

The most painful thing that Jesus ever went through was being nailed to the cross. What was Jesus thinking at that moment? Despite what he was going through, this is what he prayed: 'Father, forgive them. They don't know what they are doing' (Luke 23:34).

If Jesus could forgive those people when they hurt him the most, he can also forgive you when you do something wrong. The forgiveness we receive from Jesus gives us the power to forgive others when they hurt us. Wow!

Read More About It
in **Luke 23:34-43**.

THINK:

What is the number of legs on a chair?
What's the opposite of 'takes'?
Put them together and what do you get?
That's the word this riddle makes.

FEEL: Is there someone you need to say sorry to? Is there someone you need to forgive? Take a moment to pray and ask God to help you to make a fresh start with that person by asking for or giving forgiveness.

CREATE: Raid the recycling or find something used that needs a new lease of life. Give it a fresh start by repairing or upcycling it. Remember how God's forgiveness gives us a fresh start.

Jesus Teaches How to Pray

Bible verses: Matthew 6:8-13

Your Father knows the things you need before you ask him. So when you pray, you should pray like this:

'Our Father in heaven,
we pray that your name will always be kept holy.
We pray that your kingdom will come.
We pray that what you want will be done,
here on earth as it is in heaven.
Give us the food we need for each day.
Forgive the sins we have done,
just as we have forgiven those who did wrong to us.
And do not cause us to be tested;
but save us from the Evil One.
The kingdom, the power, and the glory are yours forever.
Amen.'

Praying is simply talking to God. It doesn't have to be complicated or full of tricky words. It's just like talking to your family or friends. You can pray anywhere, at any time, as many times as you like. God may not always answer your prayers in the way that you would like him to, but he will always listen to what you are saying.

When you pray, begin by thanking God for something. Next, say sorry to God for something you've said, done or thought that has made him sad. Then talk to God about the things you need and ask him to help you or someone you know.

Praying isn't just about having a long list of things that you would like God to do for you. Praying is as much about God talking to you as it is about you talking to God.

God can speak to you in lots of ways – through the Bible, through other people, through your heart or your mind, and through the world around you. So always be ready to listen for what God might be saying to you.

Read More About It
in **Philippians 4:6-7**.
Can you memorise these verses?

FEEL: Grab some paper and a pen and find somewhere quiet to sit down and talk to God. Ask God to speak to you and write down the things you hear him say. Remember, there are lots of different ways that God can speak to you.

GET ACTIVE: Find some red, yellow and blue paper (or any three colours), cut them into big circles and place them on the floor to use like stepping stones. When you land on a red circle, thank God for something. When you land on a yellow circle, say sorry to God for something. When you land on a blue circle, pray for something you, or someone you know, needs from God.

Jesus Preaches

Bible verses: Matthew 7:24-29

*Everyone who hears these things I say
and obeys them is like a wise man.
The wise man built his house on rock.*

From the time he was twelve years old, Jesus was teaching people of all ages about God. They were amazed by his wisdom and knowledge.

As an adult, Jesus taught many, many things that others had never heard before, especially about how to live as part of God's kingdom.

Much of his teaching was in parables, which are stories with a meaning. Sometimes the hidden meanings in his parables took a while for his disciples to work out. If you read something Jesus taught that you don't understand, ask someone older and wiser (or God) to help you to figure it out.

Jesus' most famous teaching is called the Sermon on the Mount. He sat down to give this talk in a hilly region of Galilee. It was a place that amplified his voice so that hundreds of people could hear him. (They didn't have microphones back then. You see how clever Jesus was?)

At the end of the Sermon on the Mount, Jesus tells a story about a wise person and a foolish person. A wise person is someone who not only listens to Jesus but also obeys his teaching.

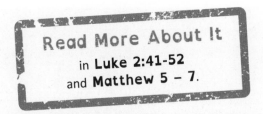

Read More About It
in **Luke 2:41-52**
and **Matthew 5 – 7**.

THINK: Read the parable of the wise man and the foolish man in Matthew 7:24-29. What did both men have in common? What was the difference between the two? Which one will you be like?

Can you spot ten differences between these pictures?

Spot the Difference

Find
10

41

Turn the page – there's more!

GET ACTIVE: Divide your family into two teams. Ask each team to build a model house from different materials.

Team 1 builds a house out of spaghetti and marshmallows.

Team 2 builds a house out of building blocks, such as Lego.

Which house is the wise man's house? You could try pouring water on them or blowing on them to see how long they would last in a storm.

CREATE: A parable is a made-up story with a meaning. Can you write a parable of your own to encourage people to listen and obey Jesus' teaching?

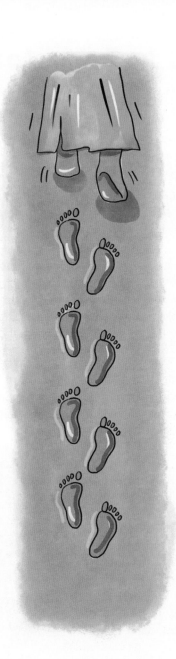

Jesus Is Transformed

Bible verses: Mark 9:2-3

Jesus took Peter, James, and John and went up on a high mountain. They were all alone there. While these followers watched, Jesus was changed. His clothes became shining white, whiter than any person could make them.

Throughout Jesus' life, people wondered who he was. Was Jesus a prophet like Elijah from the olden days? Even today, people wonder whether Jesus was really God's Son or just a good man, a holy man or even a crazy man.

Peter, a disciple of Jesus, believed that Jesus was the Christ – the Saviour for whom the Jewish people had been waiting for hundreds of years. Then Peter, along with two other disciples called James and John, saw something amazing. It was so astonishing that they weren't allowed to tell anyone about it until much later.

In an instant, Jesus was transformed (the fancy word is 'transfigured') in front of their very eyes. His clothes became dazzlingly white and two of the most important people from Jewish history – Elijah and Moses – were suddenly there, standing next to him. Then Peter, James

and John heard the voice of God saying, 'This is my Son, and I love him. Obey him!' (Luke 9:7).

After that, just as suddenly, it all went back to normal again.

Jesus was a man, but he was not *just* a man. He was also the Son of God. Those who believe in him will one day see this for themselves, just like Peter.

Read More About It
in **Mark 8:27-30**; **9:2-13**; and **Luke 9:18-36**.

FEEL: What have you learned so far in this book about Jesus that has surprised you? Is there something you didn't know and have discovered for the first time? Is there something you had forgotten and now you remember? Close your eyes and imagine what it would be like if Jesus were to suddenly appear to you in dazzlingly white clothes and a voice from heaven said, 'This is my Son!' How would that make you feel?

CREATE: Decorate a glass jar with coloured tissue paper, using either one plain piece or lots of little pieces, like a mosaic. What happens when you go into a dark room and put a small candle in the jar or shine a torch at the base of the jar? What must it have been like to see Jesus shining in all his glory?

Jesus Cares for Children

Bible verses: Mark 10:14-16

'Let the little children come to me. Don't stop them. The kingdom of God belongs to people who are like these little children. I tell you the truth. You must accept the kingdom of God as a little child accepts things, or you will never enter it.' Then Jesus took the children in his arms. He put his hands on them and blessed them.

In the Bible verses above, the disciples were trying to stop children from getting close to Jesus. They didn't want lots of them 'bothering' him, but Jesus was not happy about the disciples turning away children.

Some people believe that children are not as important as adults but that is *not* what Jesus believes. Children have a very special place in God's heart and in his kingdom. In fact, the Bible says that every child has an angel in heaven who is always with God (see Matthew 18:10).

Psalm 8:2 points out that the praises of children and babies are powerful enough to defeat God's enemies. So who wouldn't want children around?

Children have a beautiful way of seeing and exploring the world. They're able to know God's love for them and to see

God for who he really is. Grown-ups can learn a lot from children.

So, kids, take your place. Rise up and become everything that God has made you to be. Know God's blessing in your life. Don't make things complicated. Jesus loves you; he cares for you and he is with you every minute of every day.

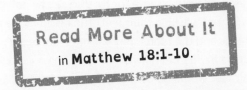

Read More About It
in **Matthew 18:1-10**.

FEEL: Close your eyes and imagine what it would be like to be hugged by Jesus. How would it make you feel? Draw a picture or write down your thoughts.

GET ACTIVE: Find a big outdoor or indoor space. Stand as far away from your grown-up as you can. Then run towards them and jump into their arms. Do this as many times as you would like.

Jesus Serves

Bible verse: John 13:14

*I, your Lord and Teacher, have washed your feet.
So you also should wash each other's feet.*

Jesus is the Son of God and has many titles, such as King, Lord, Judge and Ruler of Heaven, but he does not use his position to bully people or get his own way.

Instead, Jesus showed his love for his disciples by doing the job of a servant and washing their feet. The disciples would have worn sandals and the roads they walked were dusty – tarmac and concrete hadn't been invented yet. Can you imagine how filthy their feet would be by the end of the day?

In those days, a host would usually ask a servant to wash their guests' feet. John 13 tells us that Jesus washed his disciples' feet, showing he was not too proud to serve his friends, even when the job was a mucky one. He was not too proud to get down on his knees and help them when they needed it.

Jesus wants us to be just like him and look after one another, even when it means doing the worst jobs that no one else likes to do. When we get into a mess, Jesus is not too proud or too busy to help us.

Read More About It
in **Mark 10:35-45**.

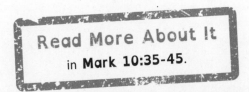

THINK: If it took Jesus two minutes to wash one foot, how long would it have taken to wash the twelve disciples' feet?

49

Turn the page – there's more!

GET ACTIVE: How many of these tasks can you do this week to serve others?

- ■ Make someone their favourite drink and give it to them.

- ■ Ask a grown-up 'Can I help you?' and then do so.

- ■ Make someone smile or laugh out loud.

- ■ Help your teacher or parent to tidy up without being asked.

- ■ Pick up some litter and put it in the bin.

- ■ Share something that's yours with a friend or sibling.

CREATE: Bake some chocolate cupcakes, decorate them, and give them away to friends, neighbours or your church family. You could even sell them to raise money for a charity or special cause. Use this simple chocolate cake recipe:

200g golden caster sugar	2 tbsp cocoa powder
200g margarine	1 tsp baking powder
4 large eggs	½ tsp vanilla extract
200g self-raising flour	2 tbsp milk

Heat the oven to 190°C (170°C for a fan oven), gas mark 5. Put all the ingredients into a bowl and mix them together until smooth. Divide the mixture into twelve cake cases and bake for fifteen to twenty minutes. Be creative with the decoration.

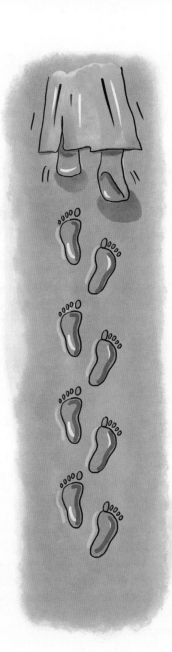

The Last Supper

Bible verses: Mark 14:22-23

While they were eating, Jesus took some bread. He thanked God for it and broke it. Then he gave it to his followers and said, 'Take it. This bread is my body.'

Then Jesus took a cup. He thanked God for it and gave it to the followers. All the followers drank from the cup.

When you read the Bible, you will find lots of times when Jesus used food and drink as a way of connecting with people. In John 6:35, Jesus called himself 'the bread of life'.

There is something very special about sitting around a dinner table and sharing food with family and friends. It brings people closer together and is a great way to talk about life. Jesus knew this, which is why he invited his disciples to a special feast.

Jesus' friends didn't fully know what was to happen later that week, but Jesus knew this was to be the last meal he would eat with them before he died on the cross. That's why it's called the Last Supper. It took place on the first day of the Feast of Unleavened Bread. It was their Passover meal (for more about this, see 'Jesus Is Crucified' on page 60).

Jesus had some very important things to say to his disciples. He introduced bread as a symbol of his body and red wine as a symbol of his blood. Then and now, Jesus was giving everyone who chose to follow him a way to remember him. That's why we eat bread and drink wine in church today. It's often called Communion and it's a great way of thanking God for all he has done for us.

Read More About It
in **Exodus 12** and **Mark 14:12-25**.

THINK: Do some research to investigate what Jesus and his disciples would have eaten at the Last Supper. (Make sure you get permission from your grown-up if you use the Internet.)

GET ACTIVE: Have a picnic (indoor or outdoor) and enjoy some of the foods that Jesus and his friends would have eaten during that meal (see the "**Think**" pathway above). Can you invite another family to join you?

CREATE: Make place mats for each member of your family. You could use paper, card, wood or corkboard. Decorate them while thinking of what you have learned about the Last Supper.

Jesus Never Gives Up

Bible verses: Mark 14:35-36

*Jesus walked a little farther away from them.
Then he fell on the ground and prayed. He prayed
that, if possible, he would not have this time of
suffering. He prayed, 'Abba, Father! You can do
all things. Let me not have this cup of suffering.
But do what you want, not what I want.'*

Have you ever had to do something important that made you
feel scared, such as taking a test in school, going to the dentist
or even having an operation in hospital? Jesus has.

Jesus prayed in the Garden of Gethsemane because he was
about to go through the most difficult thing ever. The time
had come for him to sacrifice himself
on the cross for those he loved.
He felt a deep fear that we
all, at times, might feel.
He felt it so strongly that
he wanted to give up.
He asked his Father
God whether there
was any other way to
save the world – an
easier way, a way that
meant he wouldn't
have to suffer so
much. But there was
no easy way to save

the world. This was the way that had been prepared since Eden. It was not the time to give up.

So, Jesus walked the most difficult path from the garden to the cross because he loved us so much. He was willing to do whatever it took to save us from our sins and make a way for us all to live at peace with God forever.

In the garden, Father God answered Jesus' prayer. He didn't take away the pain or make another way, but he did give Jesus the strength that he needed to face the cross and not give up.

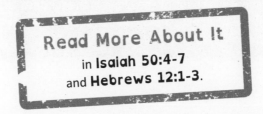

Read More About It
in **Isaiah 50:4-7**
and **Hebrews 12:1-3**.

THINK: The distance between the Garden of Gethsemane and the cross at Calvary is not very far but it was the toughest journey that anyone has ever made. Using the Bible verses below, look up the journey Jesus took between the garden and the cross – all in one night.

1. From the Garden of Gethsemane to
_____ (Mark 14:53-54).

2. Then to _____ (Mark 15:1).

3. Then to _____ (Luke 23:6-10).

4. Then back to _____ (Luke 23:11).

5. Finally to _____ (Mark 15:20-22).

Turn the page – there's more!

FEEL: Have you ever felt like giving up? As a family, talk about those times. How can you encourage one another to keep going, even when things are tough?

GET ACTIVE: Research and read about Tenzing Norgay and Edmund Hillary, the first people to climb to the top of Mount Everest. As a family, have a go at climbing a hill or a mountain. Think about which bit of the climb is the hardest. Is it the beginning, the middle or the end? What helps you to keep going? Does prayer help?

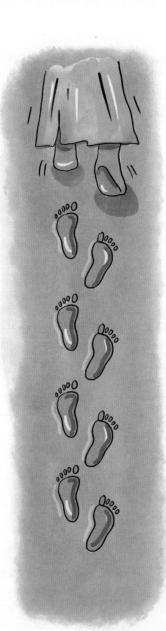

Jesus Loves You

Bible verses: John 15:12-13

This is my command: Love each other as I have loved you. The greatest love a person can show is to die for his friends.

While Jesus walked the earth, he showed love to everyone he encountered, whether rich or poor, sick or healthy. It didn't matter whether they were women, men or children, or if they were from his own culture or a different one. No one could stop him.

He showed his love in all kinds of practical ways: washing people's feet; healing their sicknesses; feeding them when they were hungry; setting them free from evil spirits; or calming a storm when they were frightened. Jesus even showed love to the Jewish leaders by telling them off when

they were behaving badly or challenging them to look at the world through God's eyes. Love isn't just a fluffy feeling. Love is an action and it comes in all shapes and sizes.

When Jesus died on the cross, it was the greatest act of love the world has ever seen. It was for everyone, for all time, and that includes you!

You can't run away from God's love. Nothing you do will ever stop God from loving you. God might not always like the choices you make but he will always love you.

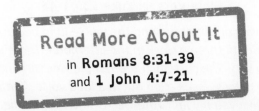

Read More About It
in **Romans 8:31-39**
and **1 John 4:7-21**.

THINK: Is there any greater way of showing love than dying to save someone? Can you think of any films in which the hero dies to save someone they love?

FEEL: What does love *feel* like? Find some objects around your house that make you think of love. It could be a special toy, a soft blanket, a candle, a photo or something else. Talk about why these things make you think of love or feel loved.

CREATE: Write a song or poem about how much Jesus loves you. Imagine Jesus singing or reading it to you.

Jesus Is Crucified

Bible verses: Luke 23:44-46

It was about noon, and the whole land became dark until three o'clock in the afternoon. There was no sun! The curtain in the Temple was torn into two pieces. Jesus cried out in a loud voice, 'Father, I give you my life.' After Jesus said this, he died.

For centuries, the Jewish people celebrated a festival called the Passover by sacrificing lambs at the Temple in Jerusalem. The blood of a lamb was a symbol of protection from God's anger at sin.

John the Baptist called Jesus 'the Lamb of God, who takes away the sins of the world' (John 1:29, NIV). He knew that, one day, Jesus would sacrifice himself for our sins so that everyone who believed in him would have eternal life.

When Jesus was crucified (that means died on a cross), it was at the time of the Passover. He took all the sins of the world – past, present and future – on his own shoulders, and they too were put to death, once and for all.

This act was so powerful that when Jesus died, the sky went dark, the earth shook and a special curtain in the Temple tore from top to bottom. This curtain symbolised the separation of the holy presence of God from sinful human beings. The torn curtain meant that Jesus had taken away our sin and we weren't separated from God any more – God did it!

Jesus died so that, by believing in him, we can have life forever with our heavenly Father God, both on earth and in heaven.

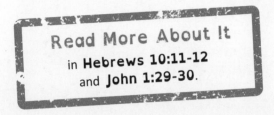

Read More About It
in **Hebrews 10:11-12**
and **John 1:29-30**.

FEEL: Dive under a blanket in the middle of the day and imagine what it was like at the moment of Jesus' death. How does it feel to know that Jesus willingly died so that you could live forever with God?

GET ACTIVE: Read 1 Corinthians 11:23-33 aloud and take Communion together as a family, according to your own tradition. For Communion, you could even try making unleavened bread, which is something Jewish people eat at Passover.

61

Turn the page – there's more!

CREATE: Unleavened bread is quick and easy to make. Try it yourself using this recipe:

1 cup plain flour
⅓ cup oil (vegetable or olive oil)
A pinch of salt
⅓ cup cold water
A little of your favourite flavouring, herbs or spices – such as rosemary and thyme or Chinese five spice – whatever you can find in the cupboard.

Heat the oven to 220°C, gas mark 7. Mix the ingredients to form a dough. Divide the dough into six balls and place them on an oven tray lined with baking paper. Press them flat and bake them in the preheated oven for ten to twelve minutes. Let them cool completely before using them for Communion with your favourite red juice.

Unleavened Bread Recipe

1 cup Flour
Flour

1/3 cup Oil

Pinch of salt

+

1/3 cup Water

= Dough

Divide dough into 6 balls, press onto prepared baking sheet

Bake at 220c 10-12 minutes

Jesus Is Alive!

Bible verses: Matthew 28:5-6

The angel said to the women, 'Don't be afraid.
I know that you are looking for Jesus, the one
who was killed on the cross. But he is not here.
He has risen from death as he said he would.
Come and see the place where his body was.'

Jesus' friends and family were terribly sad. They had watched Jesus die on the cross and they thought he was gone forever. They had forgotten that Jesus had given them clues about his coming back to life. That's why they were so shocked to see an empty grave.

Two women, both called Mary, went to the tomb to see Jesus' body three days after he had died, but it wasn't there. Instead, they were greeted by an angel who told them that Jesus was alive! How could it be true?

It wasn't until the disciples saw the risen Jesus, with the nail marks in his hands, that they believed he had miraculously come back to life. He had defeated death and done what he was sent to the earth to do.

If Jesus had stayed dead, nothing that he had said would be true. He would have been forgotten about. We wouldn't be able to be friends with God. Our sins could never be forgiven. Without the resurrection of Jesus, we wouldn't have the hope of heaven. He had to come back to life because that's what changes everything.

Christians celebrate Jesus' coming back to life at Easter time, but it's something we can celebrate every day of the year. Jesus is *alive*!

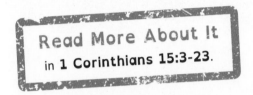

Read More About It
in **1 Corinthians 15:3-23**.

Turn the page – there's more!

THINK: Celebrate the fact that Jesus is alive by finding these words in the wordsearch:

Jesus, alive, risen, believe, celebrate, Easter, hope, resurrection, life, amazing.

Y	R	D	V	D	N	U	Z	T	D	B	R	G	Y	W
H	T	E	M	E	H	D	D	Q	Z	A	X	A	U	D
S	W	C	S	O	J	X	C	J	U	D	J	L	G	J
M	S	I	E	U	K	P	Z	T	J	O	A	I	E	A
B	R	H	H	L	R	R	J	J	E	C	G	V	A	M
B	N	X	T	P	E	R	N	N	S	U	B	E	S	X
C	X	P	O	M	G	B	E	N	U	J	H	Q	T	A
E	E	C	J	E	H	L	R	C	S	S	O	D	E	X
L	T	B	D	O	C	U	Q	E	T	L	T	I	R	P
E	Q	N	P	G	I	I	B	E	L	I	E	V	E	Z
B	K	E	F	C	L	Q	C	W	N	V	O	Z	A	E
R	X	Q	J	A	B	L	I	F	E	Z	K	N	R	E
A	A	T	C	O	M	M	Z	P	M	J	V	X	N	R
T	V	C	G	T	A	M	A	Z	I	N	G	A	M	B
E	E	L	P	C	U	Z	T	W	B	A	Z	C	G	O

CREATE: Imagine that you are a journalist or news reporter. Write and design the front page of a newspaper or film a short video, telling the world that Jesus is alive. You could even turn your bedroom into a newsroom.

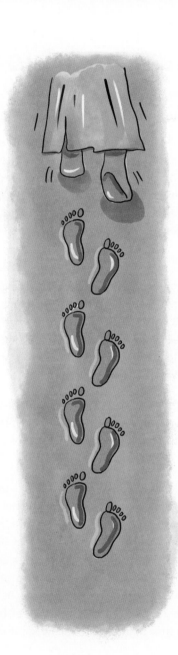

Jesus' Last Words

Bible verses: Matthew 28:19-20

So go and make followers of all people in the world. Baptize them in the name of the Father and the Son and the Holy Spirit. Teach them to obey everything that I have told you. You can be sure that I will be with you always. I will continue with you until the end of the world.

Jesus had spent much of his time on earth training his disciples to teach and preach God's message to the world. At this point in his story, he had risen from the dead and he had one last instruction to give to his disciples. It included possibly the most important words he ever spoke.

These words are known as the Great Commission: '*Go* and make followers of all people in the world.' This command wasn't just for the twelve disciples; it was for every follower of Jesus ever to live, including you.

As followers of Jesus, our mission is to tell as many people as possible about him and his amazing love for them. God loves every person on this planet and he wants them to love him too, but he won't force anyone to be friends with him. It's a choice that we make. We can show God's love to others through the things we do and say, and live in a way that is pleasing to God. Then people will see how good God is and they may want to follow him too.

Telling someone about Jesus can be scary, but God promises to be with us always. God will help you to be brave and courageous.

in **Romans 10:8-17**.

THINK: If you were to tell five people about Jesus and then each of them were to tell another five people about Jesus . . . and then each of those people were to tell five more people about Jesus, how many people would know about Jesus? How many times would you have to repeat that pattern until more than a million people knew about Jesus?

GET ACTIVE: Do you have any friends or family members who don't yet know about Jesus? Write their names on a piece of paper and pray each day that they would come to know Jesus for themselves. As a family, think of creative ways that you could tell them about Jesus. Pray for opportunities to put your ideas into action. Remember – God will help you to have courage.

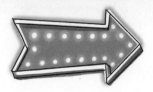

Jesus Introduces the Holy Spirit

Bible verses: John 14:16-17

I will ask the Father, and he will give you another Helper. He will give you this Helper to be with you forever. The Helper is the Spirit of truth. The world cannot accept him because it does not see him or know him. But you know him. He lives with you and he will be in you.

After Jesus had died, been buried and come back to life, it was time for him to return to heaven and take his place beside God. The disciples were sad that he was leaving, but Jesus reassured them that he would continue to be with them through the Holy Spirit.

There are many names used for the Holy Spirit: Helper, Spirit of Truth, Holy Ghost, Breath of God. He is God in the form of a spirit. He lives in us and with us.

When you choose to follow Jesus, the Holy Spirit enters your heart, mind and soul. He's a special gift from God to us. He's that gut feeling, the warmth in your heart and sometimes the goosebumps that appear on the back of your neck. He gently points out the things we do wrong so that we can get right with God. He helps us to remember the words of Jesus and understand what they mean in our everyday lives.

We might not be able to see God, but we can feel and know God with us through the Holy Spirit.

Read More About It

in **Acts 2:1-4** and find out what happened when people were filled with the Holy Spirit.

FEEL: Find a quiet space and ask God to fill you with the Holy Spirit. You might feel a deep sense of peace or a warmth in your heart. You might begin to speak in a different language. That's what happened to the people in Acts 2.

GET ACTIVE: Give each member of your family a deflated balloon. Notice how floppy and boring it is. Next, blow up the balloon and tie a knot in its neck. Notice how the balloon takes shape and seems full of life. When the Holy Spirit is with us, he breathes life and purpose into us. Have some fun with your inflated balloons.

Where Is Jesus Now?

Bible verse: Acts 7:55

But Stephen was full of the Holy Spirit. He looked up to heaven and saw the glory of God. He saw Jesus standing at God's right side.

We know that, right now, Jesus is in heaven, listening to our prayers and praying to the Father on our behalf. We know this for these reasons:

- When Jesus walked the earth, he said he would be going away to prepare a place for us in heaven.

- After he died and rose again, his physical body left the earth and went up into the clouds.

- Shortly after this, Stephen, the first person to die for his faith in Jesus, saw a vision of Jesus in heaven, standing at God's right side.

- The disciple John saw a vision of Jesus in heaven, on a glorious throne surrounded by angels and lightning, and a full, emerald rainbow.

Heaven is not a place we can see through a telescope or reach in a space rocket. It takes faith in Jesus to get to heaven and, right now, he is preparing a place for all those who believe in him.

Amazingly, even though he's in heaven, Jesus is never truly far away. His presence is always with us, through his Holy Spirit.

God the Father, Son and Holy Spirit are one and, together, they make their home with us.

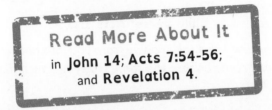

Read More About It
in **John 14**; **Acts 7:54-56**;
and **Revelation 4**.

FEEL: Jesus says that he will always be with you because the Holy Spirit is with everyone who believes in Jesus. How does that make you feel? Have there been any times when you have really needed to know that Jesus is with you?

CREATE: Design your dream home in heaven. You could use paint or modelling clay, sticks or a sketch pad — whatever you like best. What would your house be like? What colour would the walls be? Would you have furniture and a garden? Who would be there with you?

73

Jesus Will Return

Bible verse: Acts 1:11

*You saw Jesus taken away from you into heaven.
He will come back in the same way you saw him go.*

The story of Jesus is nowhere near finished.

Jesus told his disciples that even though he was going away, he would also come back. In fact, when he went up to heaven and everyone was staring at the sky, two men in white (probably angels) told them that Jesus would come back in the same way that he left.

No one knows when it will be – not even Jesus. But we do know this:

- Jesus will come unexpectedly, like a thief in the night.
- Everyone will see him.
- There will be rewards for those who wait patiently for him.
- It will be a great and glorious day.

The Bible tells us to be patient and not to give up hope. We are to keep on doing the right thing even if (or when) everyone else thinks we are crazy.

When Jesus returns, he will make everything right. The world will be renewed and transformed into something *very good*, just as God had originally planned.

Read More
About It
in **Matthew 24:27-44**;
2 Timothy 4:8;
and **Revelation 1:7**.

THINK: Read Matthew 24:27-44 and answer the following questions:

Which instrument is heard?

_____

How is the weather described?

_____

Who knows when Jesus will return?

_____

GET ACTIVE: Make up a drama where you are in the middle of doing something – such as playing at school, watching a film or washing your hair – when Jesus suddenly comes back. What would you say or do? Laugh? Cry? Panic? Sing? Faint? Try different activities and different reactions. Which one feels the most realistic?

How Can I Follow Jesus?

Bible verse: Ephesians 2:8

You have been saved by grace because you believe.
You did not save yourselves. It was a gift from God.

God loves you more than you could ever imagine. Jesus died on the cross for you, giving up his own life for yours, so that you can be friends with God forever – if you want to be. It is God's love and kindness (his grace) that saves us when we choose to believe in, live for and follow him.

If you've never made a choice to follow Jesus and you'd like to, you can pray this simple prayer:

Dear Lord Jesus,
Thank you that you love me more than I could
possibly imagine.
Thank you that you have a plan and a purpose for my life.
I know that I have done things that I shouldn't have done
and I'm really sorry.
Thank you for dying on the cross for me so that I can be
forgiven and free.
Today, I choose to give my life to you and follow you forever.
Amen.

Choosing to follow Jesus and be his friend forever is the best choice you will ever make. It will change your life. Don't forget to tell a safe grown-up (a parent, carer or church leader) about your decision to follow Jesus so that they can help you to discover more about God.